"In Quesadilla We Meet Again", is the riveting adventure of two neighbors that embark on a world wind food adventure. Bunny and Paco, are from two diverse worlds yet, they are irresistibly drawn to each other in passionate pursuit of all things Furu. The cookbook adventure of "In Quesadilla We Meet Again" explores this unbreakable bond, Paco and Bunny transcend foodie status as self-proclaimed Furu's. Paco and Bunny's food quest leads them on a fascinating path of discovery, as they fall in love with the art of food, and ultimately each other. My sincere hope is that this cookbook will bring you food, laughter, and maybe even tears. I hope "In Quesadilla We Meet Again" will warm your Cocina, and ignite your soul!

AuthorHouse™
1663 Liberty Drive
Bloomington, IN 47403
www.authorhouse.com
Phone: 1 (800) 839-8640

Because of the dynamic nature of the Internet, any web addresses or links contained in
this book may have changed since publication and may no longer be valid. The views
expressed in this work are solely those of the author and do not necessarily reflect the views
of the publisher, and the publisher hereby disclaims any responsibility for them.

Any people depicted in stock imagery provided by Getty Images are models,
and such images are being used for illustrative purposes only.
Certain stock imagery © Getty Images.

ISBN: 978-1-7283-2008-3 (sc)
ISBN: 978-1-7283-2007-6 (e)

Library of Congress Control Number: 2019910101

Print information available on the last page.

Published by AuthorHouse 09/04/2019

authorHOUSE®

INTRODUCTION

America has always had a deep affinity with food. I like to fancy the first meal as a sort of communal buffet. I try to imagine the curiosity of the Native Americans when fowl was presented. I wonder if the Pilgrims were in awe as they discovered the many uses of maze. Nowadays, we commonly refer to these comforting delights as turkey and corn. I believe this meal was the great catalyst, a preamble to the good ole U.S.A breaking bread in the spirit of comradery!

This cookbook is about finding your passion for self-exploration. Discovering your own flavor profiles. I want you to relax, no pressure. The secret weapon in this cookbook is you. The point is you don't need to be an Iron chef, or chopped champion. You are the Master of your own Culinary Cocina! Superhero of your own Kitchen! Besides, if your reading this you've already invested in the thrilling excitement of "In Quesadilla We Meet Again!". Congratulations Compadre! You have now entered the Culinary captivation of "In Quesadilla We meet Again!"

The key thing to keep in mind is this is a Spanglish cookbook. This means in these pages you will incur traditional Mexican recipes alongside my variations of tex-mex options. First, we will proceed with the basics, please, think of *"In Quesadilla We Meet Again"* as your starter guide to adlib these wonderful recipes! Customizing them to your own palate. I hope you will also peruse, and appreciate the interpretative glossary at the back of the book.

PROLOGUE

Many years ago, I had the good fortune to have a neighbor named Paco. I was always quite aware of his mild flirtations and warm Spanish eyes. Although, I was not necessarily impressed. Until one day he appeared most courageous. He approached me and said "Beautiful lady, *Mi Corazon would sing with joy if you were to come to my table for dinner*"! *I was quite fascinated by his invitation. So I graciously accepted.*

The meal Paco prepared was transcending. Paco spoke of the beauty of his country. The aroma of spices spoke to my senses while his words captured my heart. I anticipated the feast with great delight. I myself was no stranger to culinary arts, but this felt different. This experience would be life changing and I knew it.

The flavor profiles he introduced me to were titillating to the taste while pleasing to the palate. The salsa was spicy and fresh, interestingly, so was the host. Paco and I still share a love of all things culinary and would love to share these recipes with you. Needless to say, Paco is still cooking and I'm still showing up!

Allow me to take this opportunity to invite you to my table! Let me be your guide, in this adventure. We will create sumptuous creations together. Let us discover your levels of spice and heat. Some like it hot, some may like it mild. The tasty twist of this cookbook is creating your own flavor profiles as you learn. Turn the page my friend. Let us embark on this journey!

IN QUESADILLA WE MEET AGAIN

Written, produced, and food photography by **Bunny Brooks**.
Ms. Joyce Lenora Henry for being a beautiful soul.
Cover art design by **Share Faerber**.
Special thanks to **Christopher Blue** for motivational support.
Taylor Mercedes for always believing in
me and creative consulting.
Massy and **Alesha** for spiritual support.
Tim powers for just being a great human being.
Dee-de Mcglown for emotional support.

ABOUT THE AUTHOR

Bunny Brooks enjoys a colorful educational background, stemming from an early culinary arts education at Atterbury, Job Corps that she correlates with her love of food curiosity. She attributes her transitory education experience at Southwestern Illinois College of Belleville Il, with the inspiration of infusing two of her passions cooking, and writing. She is steadfast in her belief that being raised in a military environment, awakened her diversity of palate, mind, and spirit. She hopes you will continue to look forward to more *Chefstorian* accounts via *"Tango in the Noche."* The follow- up to *"In Quesadilla we Meet Again"*. She is confident, all roads will lead to culinary delights! Mrs. Brooks currently resides in Southern IL, where she continues on her culinary path, while remaining close to friends and extended family.

KEEPING IN MIND

I am quite aware many Americans are not in the wealthiest 1% tax bracket, so one of the many factor's within "In Quesadilla We meet Again" is that most of the sauces and seasonings such as *Delicioso* Valentino Mexican hot sauce, and Tajin classic Mexican seasoning are usually abundant at your local Dollar stores. I also encourage you to venture out to your local farmers market also, get some air and fresh from the farm produce fresh fruit and vegetables are essential to longevity and vitality.

I enjoy my trips to the local *Tienda or Taqueria* with Paco. I am constantly changing and evolving in efforts to eat healthier without sacrificing taste. I love the fresh air of the farmers market and supporting the natural food revolution! spending time with family and friends as we discover what is natural and ways to implement these ingredients into our rotation of daily meals. I wish you and your family many blessings and awesome safe adventures on your culinary destinations.

−Bunny Brooks

IN QUESADILLA WE MEET AGAIN

Written by *Bunny Brooks*

"In Quesadilla We Meet Again", is truly inspired by Paco's love, kindness, and dedication. I have always known Paco to be a dynamic and charismatic human being, who's love has shown me that being the best woman that I can be makes me a winner every day.

–Bunny Brooks

ABUELA'S CARNE ASADA AND FRIJOLE SOUP

(Grandmother's Steak and Bean Soup)

It was a somber spring day when I decided to visit Paco. Paco's home was only a short sprint from my own. So, I thought I'd walk. Although, it was not raining when I began my journey. I found myself in a spring shower and was dreadfully soaked by the time I reached his door.

Paco opened the door and welcomed me into the warmth of his home. It was then he said "I know just the thing to warm you, it is a soup my *Abuela* used to make when I was just a boy." Paco presented me with a bowl filled with tender chunks of steak seasoned to perfection, flanked with pinto beans in a savory stock topped with minced onion and cilantro. The meal was wonderfully filling beyond my expectations. We dined to the sound of rhythmic raindrops dancing on the roof. I was curious where this recipe came from, so I asked. Paco's amber eyes quickly became distant, I was unfamiliar with his mood. He appeared as if he were somehow transported to another place and time. Paco gazed towards the window and as the rain drops made waterfall designs on the glass he began to tell me his story. Paco explained that his mother was widowed when he and his siblings were very young. The family had to work extra hard at market to sell their fresh fruits and vegetables. The competition was very fierce with so many others vendors. The final resolve was that Paco's oldest brother had to leave school at a tender age to become the man of his *family. Paco stated because of this sacrifice he was able to remain in his studies. I saw a look of gratitude and pride embedded in his eyes, as he reflected on how hard they all worked to ends meet.*

Paco spoke of his mother taking odd jobs and his beloved Abuela holding the family together even in the face of mourning her only son. Once a week, there was bright spot. The family would pool their pesos and Abuela would go to the butcher and purchase the best cut, their pesos could buy. There would be a feast at La casa tonight! How? He did not understand how one beautiful cut of Carne asada could feed everyone. Paco struggled to concentrate on his lessons that day. He could not wait to see what his *Abuela* would create! He ran home to find his mother preparing fresh corncakes and tortillas on the outside fire. He entered his meager home to find *Abuela* stirring a savory stock filled with frijoles and spices in the kettle. He watched his grandmother prepare each essential ingredient with love. *Abuela* had always supported Paco's interest in cooking. *Abuela's* love had inspired Paco to become the chef he is today. I am very pleased that Paco shared his story and with me, so that I may pass it on to you. In retrospect, I realize on that spring day *Abuela's* soup had not just warmed my body, it had affected my soul.

Abuelas Sopa

ABUELAS CARNE ASADA AND FRIJOLE SOPA

1 lbs. chuck roast

2 cans pinto beans

1 can Jalapeños

1 medium onion

1 bush cilantro

½ teaspoon Oregano

Knorr beef powered beef bouillon

Begin with bringing 6 cups of water to a boil. Next Trim fat off edges of chuck roast. Rub on ½ teaspoon of Salt and Pepper onto Chuck Roast, now quarter the roast into ¼ pieces of medium size, place into boiling water. Let your beef cook on medium heat covered in 30 minutes Ladle off any beef residue that cooks off the beef to obtain clearer stock, continue to let simmer for an additional 30 minutes then repeat removal of any residue to achieve optimal flavor. When your broth is transparent spoon in 2 heaping tablespoons of Knorr beef bouillon powder and stir with ladle. Spoon in ½ teaspoon oregano, then pour in Pinto beans into stock add one jalapeño pepper and spoon out some carrot and jalapeño from can. Allow soup to simmer on medium heat 20 minutes. Serve with minced onion and cilantro as garnish on top.

HINT: There are plenty of onions and carrots at the bottom of jalapeño peppers in can. You may use this element to add quick spice and heat to any dish.

Blessings

HEALTHY AND HOLY GUACAMOLE

3 ripe avocados

½ cup General Ignacio's Pico De gallo

lime

Salt

Pepper

Start by cutting and halving the avocados, remove the seed. Score the inner avocado with a butter knife in a tic- tac- toe pattern. Spoon out remains onto a bowl, add in one ½ cup Ignacio's Pico de Mayo dip and gently stir until desired consistency, squeeze a twist of lime in then add a pinch of salt if desired.

NOTE TO CHEF: Your already made General Ignacio's Pico de Mayo makes this recipe faster than ever!

HINT: Try to get creative in your serving vessels for an entertaining presentation!

Healthy and Holy Guacamole!

Which came first? The avocado or the guacamole? The answer is pretty obvious. Avocados are a rich and abundant source of omega-3 fatty acids. The next aspect to consider here are the healthy benefits of enjoying guacamole. How often have you sought out for a healthy food you were actually looking forward to eating? If you listen carefully, you will hear, an angelic voice lighting your way! Oh! That's my voice! Nonetheless, your question was heard, and answered by this yummy, tummy treat crafted by *Paco*! You won't need to wait for Sunday. The recipe is about to send your taste buds on a spiritual journey.

I happen to have it on good authority that this recipe has been blessed by "Our Lady of Perpetual Avocado's." Since, we will be getting to know each other, I may as well tell you, I am a bit of a *Chefstorian*. This is a word I have coined myself, among many others'. So, you may run across my *Chefinitions within these pages*. I implore you to utilize your imagination in this lesson, it's about to get interesting. I want you to picture Adam, and Eve lounging comfortably on a rock, enjoying guacamole. If their garden was a multitude of every vegetable and fruit, why not? Sure, the vision is hilarious, right? but I am inclined to think so. After all, it was well documented that Eve was quite fond of picking fruit off trees. She certainly seems to display glowing skin and flowing tresses and at least in artist depictions. Avocados are also advertised as a key ingredient in health products also. If you like, you may continue to elaborate this topic at your next book club or wine tasting event! I feel like my place has already been reserved! Umm...yummy! Your guacamole tastes great!

GENERAL IGNACIO'S PICO DE MAYO

Hola! You may have already guessed that this lesson is inspired by *Cinco de Mayo!* *Exactamente Mi Amigo!* This colorful lesson will allow me to stretch my linguistic leg's. So, I guess you could say that I have a certain Jen ne sais quoi for communicating. Do you realize just saying *Cinco de mayo* means you are speaking Spanish already? Because *Cinco de mayo* simply means the fifth, of May, in English!

I believe the Spanish Language to be one of *Pasion*, just as I believe the French language to be one of *Amore*. This is an exciting time for me, but before I'm swept away with passion and love, we should explore what Cinco de Mayo is about. *Cinco de Mayo* commemorates General *Ignacio Zaragoza's* victory over the French on May, 5, 1862.

Every year American's migrate to their favorite local Mexican restaurants to enjoy warm weather and cold *Cerveza, food, fun, and fiesta's* follow, to celebrate this victory. You may have had indulged, in a little Margarita mayhem yourself, but don't worry, your *Secreto is* safe with me. Once you have added this recipe to your Repertoire, it sure to become the *Fiesta de resistance!* at your next *Soiree!*

This recipe is commonly referred to as Pico *de Gallo. I have chosen to honor the General with the name since he is not around to celebrate with us. You will get familiar with my Chefstorian* status throughout "In Quesadilla We Meet Again!" *Fiesta de resistance!* Is actually an example of one of my Chefinition's. (See how I did that?) Now, you can enjoy "General Ignacio's Pico de Mayo" every month now! Are you still there? Lol... I thought you were making "Pico de Mayo!"

13

GENERAL'S IGNACIO'S PICO DE MAYO

6 Roma Tomatoes

1 large white Onion

1 bush Cilantro

1 Lime

Jalapeño

Salt

Rinse all ingredient's Core and dice tomatoes, score onion to similar size as tomatoes, lay Cilantro leaves flat and chopped leaves finely, place all chopped component's in one bowl. Begin to cut Jalapeno pepper in half and remove seeds by scraping with small spoon before dicing that also., Stir with fork to mix evenly, squeeze in lime juice and then add a pinch of salt. Serves 2 to 4 people.

NOTE TO CHEF: If you enjoy the heat of the jalapeño omit scraping away the seeds and jalapeño membrane to get that Mucho caliente flavor!

THE QUINTESSENTIAL QUESADILLA

Generally speaking, the word "leftovers" alone sparks fear in our hearts. This enigma is the entire basis for the *"Quintessential Quesadilla."* If I were a superhero, leftovers would have been my kryptonite. Don't panic! "In Quesadilla We Meet Again" is your faithful sidekick. I am here to restore power in to your capable hands.

It would seem the mere sight of viewing last night's unconsumed remnant's may just trigger horror movie screams. However, the guilt of tossing leftovers away seems wasteful. This appears to be a conundrum faced by many on a weekly basis. Embracing leftovers is a daunting task in the least. This is where you the chef, can display some originality and bravado. This is your moment to shine!

When I was kiddo, I distinctly recall my mother marching out to the supper table with last nights dilapidated roast beef. That roast had seen a better day, literally yesterday! The entire time my siblings and I would chant in our most irritating voices "Are we having leftovers again?" My mother's expression resembled a prison warden serving last meals, while my father looked like a condemned man that had just been read his last rights and was wondering why someone didn't just, pull the switch! This scenario may provide comical relief, but I think we can all relate. This leads you the purpose of this chapter. You are the in essential in the *"Quintessential Quesadilla."* This lesson is about what you can bring to the table.

So what's in your Quesadilla? What is your most common leftover? Whether, it is last night's veggies or that beautiful barbequed pork or chicken you grilled? Could it be leftover rotisserie chicken? Perhaps, even that fried or smoked turkey meat? Seafood is also a strong contender. I want you to minimize these components by shredding and dicing them. Challenging yourself, to see what you can create. I want you to imagine yourself serving these delectable delights, which may become lunch, snacks, or a prelude to a side dish to main entrée. Don't forget your "Pico de mayo!" Your guest will marvel at your talent. You will be the envy of your social circle! The children will gaze at you with admiration. How clever you are!

Quintessential Quesadilla

The Quintessential Quesadilla

1 bag large flour tortillas

1 package cheddar cheese

1 cup general Ignacio's Pico de mayo

Chopped or shredded chicken

Olive oil

Warm a large flat skillet oil with olive oil on the surface, place tortilla flat on surface on low heat begin to spread shredded cheddar cheese on tortilla followed by shredded chicken add 2 tablespoons General's Ignacio's Pico de Gallo and fold over. Go to medium heat and flip Quesadilla until cheese is melted and both sides are golden brown, cut into pizza like squares and serve with Healthy and Holy Guacamole and Salsa!

Use your imagination with this one!

PACO'S AMAZING CORN

I have been fortunate enough to be a Navy Brat most of my childhood, (Navy Brat) is a term of endearment for those of us raised on military bases. This lifestyle certainly has had its advantages. Interacting with so many diverse cultures no doubt has enriched my life. Perhaps, you are alum also? Then you would know that these experiences continue to remain near and dear, to our hearts. This recipe takes me back to a time when my mother and I walked and sampled street food from different food trucks. If you are a foodie, you may have noticed the phenomena of street food has become staples on the food network scene.

If, you were not able to experience street corn which is sometimes referred to as (*Elotes* in Spanish.). Paco and I are about to bring the street corn experience to you! I hope your all ears for this lesson. All the way from Mexico to whatever territory you may currently, reside in. I would be willing to bet you didn't know, that we would be taking international trips together, so early in our friendship, did you? I get the window seat.

I believe corn to be a treasure from the heavens, it grows abundantly, and when you peel the husk you discover something beautiful! The early settler's must have thought so too! Lucky for you, one of my many talents is being a qualified Chefstorian. So, as we get to know each other you will become acquainted with my Chefinitions. I first encountered, this delicious style corn near a small community of Port Hueneme, near San Diego, California. My lovely Amiga Maria, whose, saint of a mother was kind enough to give me a taste and I been crushing on *Elotes* ever since.

I am not going to describe the taste of this one to you, or make any corny jokes. See how I did that? This recipe is super easy and you'll be sharpening your teeth on *Elotes*, faster than a kernel can pop! I want to thank you, for allowing me have the window seat in this lesson. I think we got on famously. Aww, shucks!"

Elotes

PACO'S AMAZING ELOTES

6 ears of fresh Corn

McCormick Mayonesa

1 bag Cotija cheese

1 lime

Paprika

Sea Salt

Bring large pot water to boil. While waiting on water to boil rinse off elotes and peel off husk, place in hot water let boil. Allow corn to boil 30 minutes on medium heat and then remove from water, so it may begin to cool in refrigerator for 15 minutes. Remove from fridge and cut the lime in half to squeeze the lime juice on the corn and use the lime rind to run over the kernels to permeate the lime twist! Now add Sea Salt to taste and with a butter knife slather McCormick's Mayonesa over corn on all sides then roll in Cotija cheese then garnish with Paprika and serve. Serves 2 to 6 people.

SALSA'S NOT JUST A DANCE

Picture it. You have just been seated at a crowded Mexican restaurant. Suddenly, something across the room catches your eye. Oh No! The smoke from someone's passing sizzling fajitas blurs your view. The Smoke clears. You can now focus on the thing of beauty that is moving slowly towards you. You are mesmerized and cannot take your eyes away from it.

All at once your tummy rumbles, and your mouth begins to water. You can barely control your excitement! This is the thing you have anticipated since your arrival. *Dios Mio*! Your smiling Server finally appears and announces "Salsa and Chips" The suspense has ended. You can't wait to dip those chips and taste that Salsa!

Okay, so maybe I possess a certain *"La Vida Loca"* approach to Salsa. I hope you were on the edge of your seat. I wanted you, as the *Chef, to identify with the diner*. I also wanted to convey the diner's eagerness to experience those flavor combinations. I want your family and guest be awestruck when you present *your* version of salsa. Now that we are on the same page, we can begin to explore a few fascinating particulars about Salsa.

I think it is important to mention that salsa is quickly overtaking ketchup sales in America. I think this may be the result of Americans no longer being pacified with one dimensional taste profiles. This would relegate ketchup as a one-trick pony so to speak. A new dawn of flavor possibilities is on the cusp of pioneering a new wave of condiments in our Heart's and onto our dinner tables. Salsa seems to be delivering just that!

The benefits of creating your own salsa are healthier and rewarding. I encourage you, the *Chef to* use fresh fruits and vegetables whenever possible. However, Chef always know it's perfectly fine in the spirit of time management to use substitutions. Salsa is also a plant-based food which means it is a *cholesterol free food. Something else you may want to consider is that the caloric intake from salsa is so low that it is practically non-existent. The jalapeno factor produces a powerful capsaicin component in itself that has amazing health benefits. Salsa also contains no fat all the while staying infused with flavor. Do you feel like* dancing *yet?*

Salsa

Salsa

SALSA'S NOT JUST A DANCE

6 Roma tomatoes

¼ cup cilantro

2 clove garlic

1 Jalapeño pepper

1 medium onion

Salt

Rinse off all ingredients, Roast tomatoes and jalapeño pepper on stovetop rotating them each for 2 minutes. Dice tomatoes and Jalapeño pepper into ¼ quarters, and blend until desired consistency. Pour into bowl, then dice cilantro and onion and add to bowl. Sprinkle with a dash of salt, Chill 20 minutes before serving.

NOTE: If you would like to omit heat, scrape seeds and membrane from jalapeño pepper with spoon. If you are adventurous you may opt for a Habanero or Ghost pepper!

p.s I am not that adventurous, Chef, lol….

MATADOR SOUP

In the summer of 2000, I was invited to attend a writer's symposium. Paco drove me to the airport where we exchanged our goodbye's. I returned home after a week unfortunately, so did a miserable cold. I was greeted by Paco with flowers and a much-needed hug. The next morning, I felt just awful, I phoned Paco to inform him of my status and forbade him to come over. He did not heed my warning.

Paco never blinked an eye upon encountering me in my condition. He only said "Don't worry *Senora* Paco is here now, and I will take care of you." I really did not have much of an appetite, but Paco stated that when I was ready, he would prepare a soup for me that would make me strong as the *Matadors* that face the raging bulls. I knew chicken soup was not an option with this one in the galley, I really did not know what to expect, so like a good patient I sipped my broth took my medicine and followed orders to rest until further notice.

It was day three when I awoke to the most heavenly aroma, I had begun to feel better. "Buenos Dias! Mi Amor, I hope you are well enough to join me in the *Cocina* today." I was finally seated at the breakfast nook when Paco placed a large bowl of aromatic soup on the table. I was overwhelmed by the beauty of this soup! It looked to magnificent to eat, but to delicious not to! This Veggiephoria experience was so stellar, the only stars I was seeing were the ones in Paco's eyes. Be ready to star in your own "Matador Soup" romance with this recipe. *Cuidado*! It is a steamy dish. Oh! Let's get back to the recipe? (lol…) Chef.

This soup consists of carrots, shredded cabbage, and chayote squash, zucchini and tiny red potatoes all simmering in a tantalizing stock, bursting with herbs, tender chunk of beef covered beneath the cabbage, minced onion, and cilantro. When my parents told me to eat my veggies they never looked or tasted this delicious! "Matador Soup" contains nutrients vital to the body that you cannot get out of a can. Paco's "Matador Soup" can be enjoyed anytime you like! It's all up to you if you wish to share the recipe! Better yet, tell them to get their own copy. Lol… lucky, for you my friend, Paco and you are on a first name basis! Enjoy!

Matador Soup

Large stock pot

1 poblano pepper

1 jalapeño pepper

3 lbs. beef shanks or oxtails

4 peeled carrot

1 Zucchini

2 Cloves garlic

1 chayote squash

4 baby red potatoes

Knorr beef powdered bouillon

1 head of cabbage

Cilantro

Place beef in 6 cups of boiling water alone for 30 minutes. Skim off any residue at top continue to let beef boil another half hour then repeat skimming process. (A clearer broth is a better tasting broth.) Slice cabbage into strips and zucchini into chunk (set aside to add in the stock last) add in 2 heaping tablespoons bullion powder, proceed to add garlic, potatoes, chopped cilantro and Jalapeño to broth then add salt and pepper to taste. Allow these components to simmer another 20 minutes then add sliced cabbage and chopped zucchini and problemo pepper on top of stock cover and simmer on medium heat until meat is tender and falling apart. Top with diced onion and cilantro squeeze lime over soup, if desired.

NOTE: Chef, if more heat is desired then add Habanero pepper to broth.

RIB'S EL NORTE

It was the winter of 2006, Paco and I were Chicago bound for our first road trip. I was not a fan of highway travel, so I was experiencing much trepidation. The negative temperatures did nothing to quiet my anxieties. Paco reassured me of a safe trip, so I climbed in his truck and off we went. We had managed to arrive ahead of the schedule. When we reached our destination it became abundantly, clear that we were grounded for the night. Due to the white out conditions.

We were greeted with concern, as we were informed of a pending snowstorm. Paco and his brothers declared that they were going out to reach the local Tienda for supplies. I was hesitant to let him go, but he quashed my distress by saying "A blizzard cannot stop me from returning to you, it may only slow me down."

I watched out the window, as his truck blended into the bleached landscape then vanished. I managed to measure my time in his absence by maintaining the fire and sipping warm cocoa. Paco did return, then he disappeared into the Cocina. When Paco resurfaced he announced that dinner would soon be served. Paco gestured for me to sit next to him, "Come Senora, let the fire warm you" he said softly.

He tossed another log into the fire, it crackled loudly as if it were trying to compete with the sinister howl of the wind outside. We watched solemnly, as the ember's floated and danced into absentia. Dinner was eventually served and I was blessed enough to be presented with a wonderful meal that featured Paco's tender, lip-smacking beef rib's slathered in a robust sauce, served on a bed of Spanish rice with Frijoles negros crumbled with Cotija cheese. Amid all the commotion, I had simply forgot how famished I was! But, barbeque in a blizzard?

Had I become, a ribs in the winter convert? I most certainly did! I am hoping to make you a believer also!

Paco wants you to know his "Rib's El Norte" recipe is versatile and works on the grill too! You can enjoy "Ribs El Norte" all year round! But, if you get a hankering for some ribs on those cold winter evenings start your ovens. Paco and I want you to have your own "Rib's El Norte" experience and don't forget to pair your ribs with your choice of wine, you can always wash the sauce off those fancy glasses tomorrow. Carpe Diem! Chef, after all, it's a blizzard outside!

Ribs El Norte

3 lbs. beef ribs

3 tablespoons Liquid smoke

1 teaspoon steak sauce

1 tablespoon Heinz 57

1 tablespoon Spicy mustard

1 teaspoon Soy sauce

2 tablespoon Worcestershire sauce

¼ cup Brown sugar

Preheat oven to 300 degrees. Line cooking tray with foil. Douse ribs well with liquid smoke, rub in to permeate smoky flavor. In a large bowl mix steak sauce, soy sauce, Worcestershire sauce, and spicy mustard then stir until blended. Marinate ribs a minimum 30 minutes or overnight. Before placing in oven coat the top of the rib's with brown sugar pressing the brown sugar into the ribs Heat at 300 degrees for 3 hours or until done. Drain fat off garnish with Heinz 57 sauce and enjoy!

Bonus! Bunny's Boss sauce

1 bottle Honey flavored barbeque sauce

1 cup Valentina hot sauce

1 lime

½ cup water

Cracked black pepper

Slice lime in half first, combine all ingredients in sauce pan over low heat, simmer on low until sauce begins to bubble the add half slice jalapeño for heat (Optional)

ROJO DE CALIENTE CHICKEN WINGS

Have you ever eaten hot wings so outstanding, you've pictured yourself wearing a bib? Granted, visualizing this image may provide you with a hearty chuckle. Hot wings are meant to be a little messy, remember? Hot wings were created as an appetizer at a social function in the late 1960s. Subsequently bursting into popular culture throughout the 1980s. Many franchises have built their entire business model around chicken wings and in the process, the commercial style hot wings have lost allure and appeal. I am sure like myself, you have tried most of them.

      I don't know anyone who does not enjoy a superb hot wing, I am no different. I found myself in a kind of wing coma. The restaurant wing's I frequently consumed were not putting me to sleep, but they were not waking me up with flavor either. My own hot wing recipe needed resuscitation, and I knew just the chef to help me breathe life into it. So, my quest for a fiery hot wing lead me into Paco's *Cocina*. This delicious hot wing recipe will reveal to you, how you can permeate flavor into those wings. Beware, Chef! This recipe is going to end with a secret twist! Come, follow me into hot wing nirvana! When you discover the hidden message in this recipe, you will know, when you have struck gold! The only challenge left is keeping "Rojo de Caliente" wings from flying off your serving plate!

Rojo De Caliente Wings

3 lbs. fresh chicken wings

1 bottle Tajin seasoning

1 bottle Valentina hot sauce

1 stick butter

1 canola oil

Pre heat your oven to 250 degrees. In a large bowl, marinate wings in one cup Valentina and Tajin Mexican seasoning hot sauce a minimum of half-hour. Place wings on baking sheet for 20 minutes bake wings then remove them from oven while they rest, begin to heat cooking oil. Drop wings into hot oil until they float and are somewhat crisp. Allow wings to cool while you heat butter on low setting while adding 1 cup of your favorite choice of hot sauce to the butter heat until melded then liberally pour sauce over wings and serve with celery and ranch dressing in the side.

The twist in Rojo de Caliente wings is that you are the factor here in your final taste and flavor! Americans love hot sauce, and adding your own favorite rather it be Frank's red hot or Louisiana to Tabasco, you are the final decision maker here! Don't forget to have cold one to wash down those awesome wings!

BEEFING WITH ME

What if you could have all your favorite things bundled into one delicious meal? Well, you can with my tex-mex burrito recipe! This lesson is inspired by millennials. This generation is always on the go, and desires that instant gratification of convenience. Bundling is all over the television and seems to be the bee's knees of multi-tasking nowadays. So, why not apply this mindset to Furu status. We can, and we will.

My me-maw once told me that life, is about squeezing all the good stuff in before it ends. When something is good, we never want it to end. Luckily, for you we have become *Dos Amigos* from the moment you opened *"In Quesadilla We Meet Again!"* I am *Muy Feliz* to share my Deliciosa recipe with you. My younger family members refer to my burritos as (Lit... refer to nearest youngster to get said definition. (lol...) Keep in mind that it is the Chefs prerogative to use ground turkey, chicken, or lamb, meat in your recipe, these are all viable options in this recipe.

If you think your dinner guest may be interested in a tortilla stuffed with meat, refried beans, and overflowing with *Queso* inside a soft flour tortilla shell, topped off by lettuce, "Pico de mayo" and sour crema, then we are *Simpatico*. Get ready for your *familia* to shout *"Muchas Gracious"* when these *burritos* are rolled out to your dinner table.

43

Millennials

Beefing with me

1 pkg. flour tortillas shells

1 Pkg. Monterrey jack cheese

1 pkg. sharp cheddar cheese

1 pkg. 2 lbs. hamburger meat

1 pkg. Taco seasoning ()

1 can refried beans

Brown ground beef first, drain fat from beef then add taco seasoning to beef. When this is prepared just as if you were making tacos, turn heat down to low heat and spoon in refried beans from can. Pour one cup of water into mixture over medium heat and slowly stir allowing them to meld, Remember, air on the side of moistness because you want that cheese to melt accordingly. Once your burrito mixture is the consistency you desire, season mix to desired taste, turn off heat let mixture rest. Warm tortillas in oven until flexible., lay out tortilla then spoon desired mix onto tortilla and then spread cheese on top of burrito mixture. Fold the bottom of shell up first, then the top the side and roll into your burrito. Heat in oven at 425 degrees for ten minutes Serve with sour creama lettuce and salsa.

NOTE: If you would like to make your burritos freezer ready then lay out single sheets of foil to wrap your Burritos in when done. Hint: some foil comes already cut in separate squares to expedite rolling. This makes for quick meals.

VEGGIE FAJITAS

Attencion! Hermanas Y Hermanos. You may recall those sizzling *fajitas* that passed you in the salsa chapter. The next time you see those *Fajitas* you will be the one serving them! I suggest you invest in some Fajita skillets; you may find them online or at your local marts easy enough. I like to do one skillet placed on the midst of the table, so skeptics can get a bird's eye view of the goodies, let's introduce these seasoned veggies to the palate in a way no one can resist!

This Veggiephoria experience is served in many fine establishments. Today, they will be served in yours, if you can get them to table, without deciding to treat yourself in the kitchen. This recipe makes for an exciting presentation and even better for healthy unprocessed food. I simply adore your tenacity! You have become quite the Chefantic through these pages. Remember, Chef that it is *Muy importante* that you familiarize yourself with your choice of veggie's. I want you start off with my recipe then later adlib your own favorites and seasonings.

When you are comfortable with your *Fajita* skills, you may then incorporate shrimp, marinated beef slices, or chicken to suit your specific taste. This no meat treat is sure to be a fan favorite for all. I am sure your Chefstorian account of how you mastered this *Fiesta de resistance* will be a story to tell, but then again, I knew you were awesome from the moment we shared chips and salsa!

Veggie Fajitas

Veggie Fajitas

2 stalks Broccoli

1 head of Cauliflower

1 large white Onion

1 Tajin seasoning

1 red bell pepper

1 green bell pepper

1 yellow bell pepper

Salt

Pepper

Rinse all vegetables, begin by cutting Cauliflower into smaller component's and Broccoli into florets keeping separate. Halve all 3 bell peppers and take out centers, then slice bell peppers into thin medium thin slices, do the same with onion. Begin to oil skillet of choice and place on stovetop to heat, when heated put in cauliflower first and let the cauliflower stir-fry for five minutes. After Cauliflower begins to brown add in Broccoli and systematically add other component's, turn down high heat and sprinkle on Tajin and a pinch of salt to taste rotating vegetables to get seasoning on them and cover on medium heat continue to cook this way for five minutes then pour 1/3 cup water into mix and recover turning off the heat underneath to allow stem under lid to continue to sauté flavor into the veggies.

NOTE TO CHEF: While I do recommend purchasing a Fajitas skillet I like to transfer my cooked veggies onto the skillet before I bring them out and allowing them to cool down and the fajita skillet to remain room temperature for safety.

FRUTA LA PLAYA

I had taken up residence in the Midwest for many years, and it was a wonderful place, Southern California is my home state but, there were times, when I became homesick. I longed for the fresh ocean air and the cool sand beneath my feet. My melancholy did not go unnoticed by Paco. I just happened to be on hiatus that week, when Paco suggested an impromptu vacation to Myrtle Beach, South Carolina. He didn't have to ask me twice. I packed quickly, and we boarded our flight, I was so excited! Sure, the Pacific Ocean was obviously my first love, but I figured I had room on my dance card for a tango in the Atlantic.

We arrived at our hotel which displayed a panoramic view of emerald green rolling waves that at times appeared to be a majestic grey. Paco and I wasted no time getting down to the boardwalk. The giant ferris wheel was a sight to see! We spent the day wandering in and out of shops, arcades, and eateries of course. Paco insisted that I boogie board on the waves, but I reminded him that I was more of a boogie dancer, than a boogie boarder. I recall this time vividly, as I watched Paco drift on the waves, his smile shimmering like the warm iridescent sun that graced the translucent waters. During our time in Myrtle Beach, time moved quickly yet, seemed to inexplicably stand still.

By night we walked the boardwalks and took in the night life. Paco managed to get a guitar from some unknown source. In the evenings, he found us a spot on the beach and lay a blanket and sang to me under the stars. He played the guitar badly, but in Paco's defense, I reminded myself the man is a chef not a musician, p.s. I hope he doesn't read this chapter... lol... others joined us and the nights were magical, but honestly, what wasn't magical when I was with Paco?

The last night of our vacation Paco requested I wear a beautiful red dress, he purchased for me at one of the shops. I told Paco I wanted to save it for a special occasion to which he replied "Every day with you *Senora* is *especial*, we will order room service and dine on the patio tonight, I do not want to share you tonight, *Mi Amor*." Paco and I dined on a wonderful four-star meal. We then sat and watched the lights from the colossal wheel and we could faintly hear some music.

Paco turned to me and said "I have a surprise for you, *Senora*." Paco disappeared and came back revealing a rather large champagne glass filled with watermelon, cantaloupe, grapes, and strawberries once again a work of art! Suddenly, Paco appeared to have dropped something and when I stood, he said softly "Stay as you are right now *Senora,* so that I may always remember the way you look this very moment!" Paco held out his hand to reveal a diamond ring. Paco proposed to me right then and there! Pondering my response, I was suddenly aware of the sound of the waves crashing, and the wind whipping my hair wildly, the seconds must have seemed like an eternity to Paco. I am saddened our journey has to end here, we have become so close, Chef, since you first opened *"In Quesadilla We meet Again."* We have become good friends. Do not fear. The culinary adventure of Bunny and Paco will continue! You may look forward to that in *"Tango in the Noche."* The follow up to ''In Quesadilla We Meet Again" until then farewell, and *Mochas Besos Chef!*

Fruta La Playa

Blueberries

Grape's

Watermelon

Pineapple

Strawberries

Cantaloupe

Lemon

Tropical Disposition
(Not Optional)

Wash all fruit off, then chop into desired sizes and serve in vessel of choice. Top with grapes Squeeze lemon over top and enjoy accordingly!

HINT: you may serve Fruta la Playa over pound cake or with whipped cream, maybe even cottage cheese for a really healthy snack! You may also incorporate your favorite fruit in also, get creative!

GLOSSARY

Abuela* Grandmother

Amigo* Companion

Amour* French word for love

Attention* Attencion

Beso* Kiss

Bravado*Boldness

Buenos Dias! Good morning

Burrito* A Mexican originated tortilla filled with ingredients of one own choosing.

Carne asada* Marinated beef Mexican style

Carpe diem* Seize the moment

Cervesa* Beer

Chefanitic* Fanatic of cooking.

Chefinitions* Definitions of a chef.

Chefstorian* A chef personal account of how a particular food came to be

Cuidado* Care

Dios mio* Oh my God!

Dos* two

Fiesta de resistance* Party of all parties.

Cilantro*Coriander leaves commonly used in Mexican dishes.

Cinco de mayo* A celebration on the fifth of may recognizing Mexico victory over the French in 1862.

Corazon* Heart

Cocina* Kitchen

Cotija* A cow's milk cheese originated in Mexico.

Compadre* A way of addressing a friend.

Delicioso* delicious

Elotes* ears of corn

El Norte* The North

Especial* Special

Exactamente* Exactly

Familia* Family

Fiesta de resistance* Best of the best.

Frjioles* Beans

Frjioles negros* Black beans

Fruta la Playa* Fruit at the beach

Foodie* A person that has interest in culinary arts.

Furu* food guru

Guacamole* mashed avocado with other ingredients.

Habanero* A very hot chili pepper.

Hasta luego* See you later.

Hermana's* Sister's

Hermano's* Brother's

Hola* Hello

Fantastico* Fantastic

Fajitas* A dish of Mexican origin usually served with vegetables and meat *

Jalapeno* A chili pepper pod that cultivates capsicum.

Je na sais quoi* A quality or talent that is that is undescribed.

La casa* Home, House

La vida loca* Living crazy

Lit*Feeling of euphoria, nirvana, happiness.

Maize* Corn

Matador* A skilled bullfighter

Me maw* Grandmother

Mi Amor* My love

Millennials* Generation Y

Mucho gracias*Many Thanks

Mucho Caliente* Very Hot

Muy feliz* Very Happy

Muy importante* Very Important

Noche* Night

Peso* Mexican currency

Pico de Gallo* A mix of onion, cilantro, and tomato

Pasion* Passion

Repertoire* A set skill set one may attain.

Salsa* Spanish word for sauce

Secreto* Secret

Senior* Mr.

Senora* Woman

Soiree* French for party or gathering.

Sopa* Soup

Sour crema* Sour cream

Simpatico* Agreement

Tango* A dance originated in the 1980's in Rio La Pata002E

Tienda* Store

Taqueria* Mexican restaurant specializing in taco and burritos

Tex-Mex* A style of cooking formed in the Southwest.

Queso* Cheese

Quesadilla* A heated tortilla with cheese.

Quintessential* Necessary

Repertoire* Skills set that a preparer knows or performs habitually.

Veggiephoria* Euphoria over vegetables